Georges Gromort

SMALL STRUCTURES

French Architecture
of the Early
Nineteenth Century

VNR VAN NOSTRAND REINHOLD COMPANY
_____ *New York*

Printed in the United States of America
Designed by Loudan Enterprises

Van Nostrand Reinhold Company Inc.
115 Fifth Ave.
New York, New York 10003

Van Nostrand Reinhold Company Limited
Molly Millars Lane
Wokingham, Berkshire RG11 2PY, England

Van Nostrand Reinhold
480 La Trobe Street
Melbourne, Victoria 3000, Australia

Macmillan of Canada
Division of Canada Publishing Corporation
164 Commander Boulevard
Agincourt, Ontario M1S 3C7, Canada

16 15 14 13 12 11 10 9 8 7 6 5 4 3 2 1

Library of Congress Cataloging-in-Publication Data

Gromort, Georges.
  Small structures.

  Bibliography: p.
  Includes index.
  1. Architecture, Modern—19th century—France.
2. Architecture—France. 3. Architecture—Composition, proportion, etc. I. Title.
NA1047.G76   1986   720′.944   85-20196
ISBN 0-442-22989-5

Small Structures

Contents

Foreword to the French Edition—1953

The work of today's architects is characterized by a sense of simplicity linked with a revival of interest in the designs of a past that our immediate predecessors chose to ignore, chiefly because of its lack of ornamentation. It is this very economy of design and composition that we now find so attractive however, especially the works of certain architects of the Directoire and of those who survived the First Empire without forgetting that the teachers of their youth had been contemporaries of Gabriel and Louis. These works, then, for all their simplicity, have a breathtaking elegance that makes them ideal examples for our own time. For their simplicity is neither dogma nor weakness, neither superficiality nor puritanism—it is restraint and sheer good taste. This is not to say that these architects were ignorant of the effects created by the somber, majestic ornamentation of Louis XVI; rather, they deliberately chose to tread a less obvious path to success.

Here we find facades where simple windows give the only relief in broad sweeps of masonry. It may be that they were richly decorated in the beginning and that the architect gradually whittled away the ornamentation as he realized how little it accorded with the overall scheme of his plans. These designs may look as if they were made to be richly decorated—and we may suppose that they were harder to simplify than they were to overload—but they are still more impressive than others in which simplicity is a goal in itself, for simplicity loses aesthetic value when devoid of contrast.

We believe the time is right to publish a modest collection of some of these works from the late eighteenth and early nineteenth centuries. Many are projects actually realized by artists such as Bélanger and Ledoux, while others have been carefully copied and enlarged from the less familiar collections of Seheult and Charles Normand. The following bibliography gives the sources from which these "little houses" have been taken.

Georges Gromort, 1953

Bruyère, L. *Etudes relatives à l'Art des constructions.* 2 vols., Folio. Paris: Bance, 1828.

Gourlier, Biet, Grillon, et Tardieu. *Choix d'Edifices publics, projetés et construits en France depuis le commencement du dix-neuvieme siècle.* 3 vols., Folio. Paris: Louis Colas, 1825 and 1836.

Krafft. *Maisons de campagne, habitations rurales, etc.* Folio. Paris: Bance, 1849.

Ledoux, Ch.-N. *L'Architecture considerée sous le rapport de l'art, des moeurs et de la législation.* Paris: published by the author, 1804 (2 vols.), and Paris: Daniel Ramée (3 vols.), 1847.

Normand, P.-Ch.-J. *Recueil variés de plans et façades, motifs pour des maisons de ville et de campagne, des monuments et des établissements publics et particuliers.* 1 vol., folio with 50 plates. Paris: published by the author, 1825.

Percier and Fontaine. *Palais, maisons et autres édifices de Rome moderne, dessinés à Rome 1798.* 75 plates, large folio. 1802.

Seheult, F.-L. *Recueil de divers motifs d'architecture dessinés en Italie dans les anneés 1791, 1792 et 1793 par F.-L. Seheult, architecte à Nantes.* (Published from 1811).

Foreword to the German Edition—1981

We fell in love with these pages long before we began to study them critically, and that was our first reason for publishing them. Gromort's slim volume was a chance discovery made in a secondhand bookshop in Paris. We have since guarded it jealously and only lent it to friends working on new projects or competitions, not so much by way of example, but more as an inspiration and happy stimulus to the design and creation of town houses— a form that has come back into fashion as a somewhat ironic footnote to the themes of Postmodernism and Historicism.

Critical examination eventually revealed the book's true content, of course: a serious typology of ground plans from which one may learn, but not copy, and a romantic contradiction in the facades, one of which Gromort alludes to in his own Foreword and which arises out of a temptation to, but renunciation of, excessive ornamentation. But all these things are seen on closer inspection.

The initial impression is one of similarity between these studies, dating from around 1800, and designs that have carried off many a prize in recent competitions in Berlin. This is no coincidence: the liberation of architecture from a dearth of forms led in many instances to a confused and misunderstood plethora of shapes which, copied and reassembled merely for their own sake, are devoid of any sense of order or of feeling for our age. As Gromort himself says, simplicity for its own sake forfeits aesthetic value, for it is empty of contrast. By the same token, today's stock of received ideas and forms has little worth in and of itself— there is nothing great in copying Palladio. In architecture, anything might serve as an example—history, genius, nature, or technology can all be transformed, seriously or ironically, into whatever we like or whatever is in demand. But transformation with a "personal touch" and as a result of genuine necessity— this is essential.

How different are the plaudits of simplicity that Gromort heaped on these designs in 1953 from the associations of ideas we get when looking at them in 1981. The book would surely elicit yet a different reaction if reissued in the year 2011. The pages themselves remain untainted by any interpretation.

Monsieur Gromort added a few notes to his collection, and we reproduce these without comment, since it is the drawings that are important and not any purely archival interest. Sources are given for architects or readers wishing to delve deeper.

Martina Düttmann, 1981

SMALL STRUCTURES

François-Joseph Bélanger

1744–1818

Bélanger was architect to the Comte d'Artois, an outstanding post that afforded him access to a wide aristocratic clientele, even though Bélanger's work came at a time when the wealthy were devoting themselves passionately to the redesigning of gardens. It can almost be said that he was compelled to specialize in the kind of architecture that provided the fashion of the age every opportunity to surround itself with pastoral or Anglo-Chinese gardens. For this reason his name is linked with creations such as *Beloeil, Mérévillee, Folie-Saint-James,* or the *Pavillon de Bagatelle*. A student of Brogniard, Bélanger appears to have been more sensitive than his tutor and continued to represent the *Belle Epoque* of Jacques-Ange Gabriel during the regency of Louis XVI. His architecture is everywhere restrained, refined, and lucid.

Plate I: Maison à Pantin

This "country house" was designed by Bélanger for an American, Mr. de la Ballue, and was erected in 1785. The tiny plot of land left hardly any room for a garden, and the architect had to summon all his skill to find room for paths and a small lawn laid out "in the middle of a terrace that forms a semicircle around the courtyard above the coach houses and stables and on a level with the first-floor apartments." Behind this semicircle, records Krafft, who published the designs for this extraordinary house, were mature trees that afforded privacy and shade for the terrace, which was approached over a bridge from the salon.

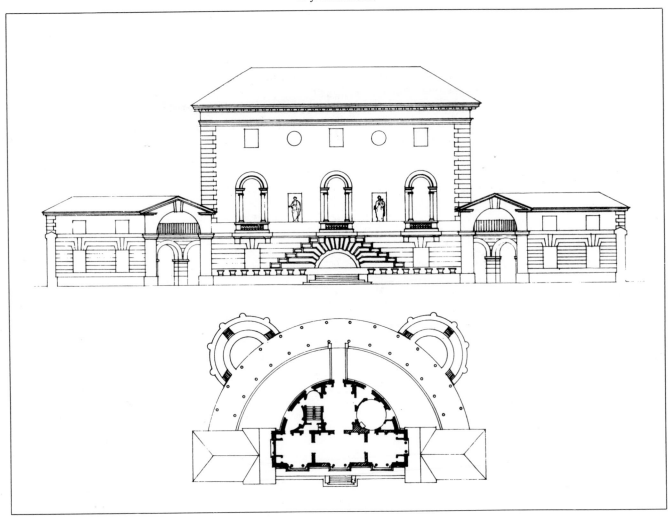

MAISON A PANTIN (1785).

Plate II: Pavillon de Bagatelle
Front entrance
The *Pavillon de Bagatelle* was built in a mere sixty-four days during 1778 to win a wager struck by the Comte d'Artois. However, the drawings published by Krafft show that the Comte's "madness" was well tempered by the structure we see today, completely rebuilt by Sir Richard Wallace during the Second Empire. The property is superbly well proportioned, and the enclosures to the pavilion and the layout of the large, beautiful, English landscape garden are quite simply masterful.

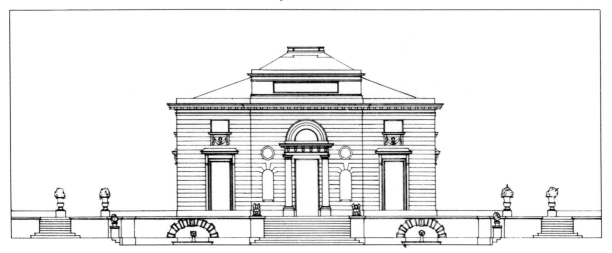

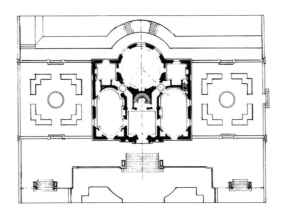

PAVILLON DE BAGATELLE (FOLIE D'ARTOIS)
(ÉTAT PRIMITIF)

Plate III: Pavillon de Bagatelle
Rear facade
This facade is not as well proportioned as the entrance facade. There is something heavy in the mass of stone that weighs down upon the arched windows of the great salon. This view is given merely to amplify the impression gained from Plate II.

Plate III: Pavillon de l'Hotel de Brancas
This pavilion was designed by Bélanger for the Comte de Lauraguais. The front view shown here is typical of the artist and his skill in retaining the elegance of a previous epoch beneath the stern lines that fashion then dictated.

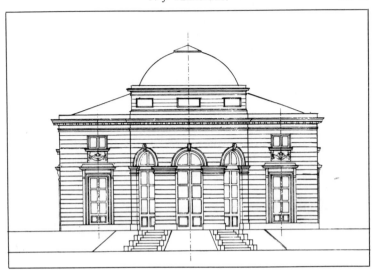

PAVILLON DE BAGATELLE - FACE POSTÉRIEURE

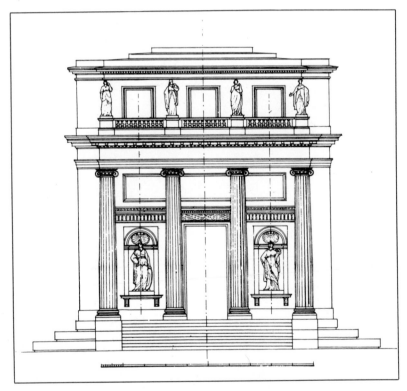

PAVILLON DE L'HÔTEL DE BRANCAS

L. Bruyère
Inspecteur Général des Ponts et Chaussées

Bruyère, a man of taste and sensibility, published several works, including one in two volumes entitled *Etudes Relatives à l'Art des Constructions*. Volume II contains a series of drawings that the author dubbed "plans of a number of buildings for the village × 2." The drawings could be regarded as an early attempt at urban planning in the countryside, much of which still applies today. Plates IV, V, and VI are taken from this section.

Plate IV: Presbytère pour le Village de X.
According to Bruyère, the rectory is clearly laid out and restrained in appearance, incorporating a small school in addition to apartments for priests and the vicar.

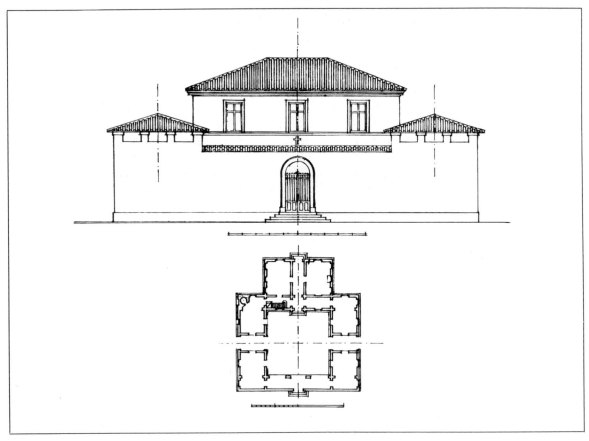

PRESBYTÈRE, POUR LE VILLAGE DE X.

Plate V: Chapelle Sépulcrale
This cemetery chapel was meant to be erected at the entrance to the cemetery for funeral masses. The design is exemplary in its simplicity of line and in the abundant clarity of purpose in ground plan, view, and section.

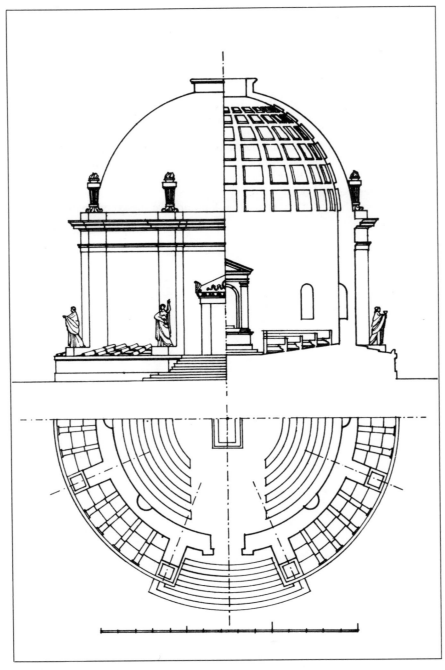

CHAPELLE SÉPULCRALE

Plate VI: Maison de Ville
A distinguishing feature of this town hall—also designed for the village of X—is that the first floor is devoted to the tasks of the local magistrate, while the mayor, whose role is mainly that of a figurehead, is relegated to the second floor. Both floors are designed to be open on the entrance side; hence the split-level, covered staircase that dictates the frontal design. The ground floor accommodates the large courtroom, two offices, the chancellery, and a guardroom. Upstairs are the council chamber and a number of offices.

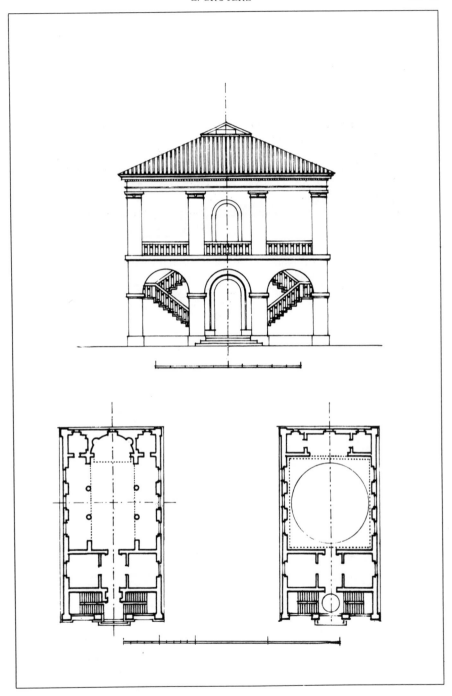

MAISON DE VILLE

Jean-François-Thérèse Chalgrin

1739–1811

Chalgrin was born in Paris and was a pupil of Jean Nicolas Servandoni. In 1758 he was awarded the Grand Prix d'Architecture, and in 1770 he became a member of the *Académie d'Architecture*. To him we owe the church of *Saint-Philippe-de-Roule* and the north tower of *Saint-Sulpice*, but he is chiefly remembered for the design of the *Arc de Triomphe*, the erection of which also began under his direction.

Plate VII: Pavillon de Madame Elisabeth à Versailles
This pavilion, with its many obliques in ground plan, is reminiscent of the *Pavillon Français* built by Gabriel in Trianon in 1750. The architectural conception is light and airy, but we must acknowledge Krafft's criticism that the angled walls are little suited to the wall decoration for which they were intended.

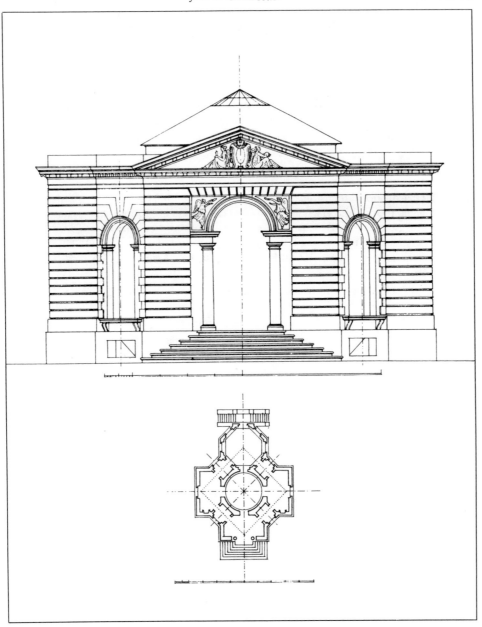

PAVILLON DE MADAME ÉLISABETH, A VERSAILLES

Jean-Michel Dalgabio

1788–1852

Born in Rive (Piedmont), Dalgabio later took French nationality; he was a student of Delespine and the architect of the city of St. Etienne.

Plate VIII: Corps de Garde et Octroi
Guardroom and customs office—a complex combination to which Dalgabio found this very skillful answer. The letters in ground plan mean: A—guardroom; B—customs office; C—common entrance hall; D—sergeant's office; E—cell; F—customs inspector; G—storeroom; H—washrooms. (Plates VIII and IX are taken from *Choix d'Edifices Publics* by Gourlier.)

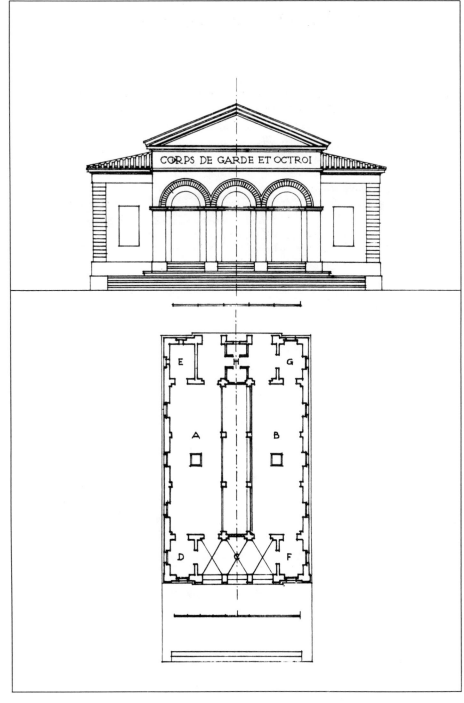

CORPS DE GARDE ET OCTROI, A SAINT-ÉTIENNE (1816)

Alphonse-Henri de Gisors

1796–1866

De Gisors was the nephew of Alexandre de Gisors and a student of Charles Percier. Like his uncle before him, he was an *Inspecteur Général des Bâtiments Civils* and joined the *Académie* in 1855. His name is associated with works for Luxembourg, especially the *Chambre des Paris*, which later became the Senate.

Plate IX: Corps de Garde de Pompiers
This small fire station, designed in 1828, was located in Paris in the Rue Mouffetard, forming the angle between two oblique streets. It was certainly impressive in its harmonious composition, despite its small size—the entrance facade was a mere 11.5 meters long.

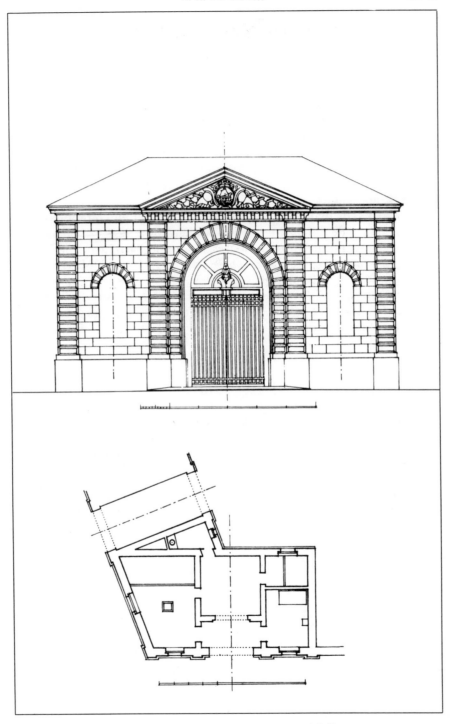

CORPS DE GARDE DE POMPIERS, A PARIS (1828)

Charles Nicolas Ledoux

1736–1806

Ledoux was born in Dormans and was a student of Jacques-François Blondel, joining the *Académie d'Architecture* in 1773. Ledoux built a number of town houses for the aristocracy in Paris and Eaubonne and designed many of Paris' city gates, of which the rotunda of *La Villette,* the kiosk on the *Place Denfert-Rochereau,* and the columns on the *Place de la Nation* still stand. The theater at Besançon is one of the few major commissions that was actually constructed; many of his projects were never implemented. These include fascinating plans for a new town near the Chaux salt mines and the customs houses all around Paris, which were unfortunately rejected as a *mur murant Paris.* He published his work, with a dedication to Tsar Alexander I of Russia, in five volumes entitled *L'Architecture Considerée sous le Rapport de l'Art, des Moeurs et de la Legislation.* The first two volumes appeared in 1804; the other three did not come out until long after his death in 1847.

Plate X: Hôtel de Monsieur Tabary
This town house was situated in the *Rue Faubourg-Poissonière* and appears in the second volume of his work. As with most of his private villas, the style is Italianate rather than Greek. His propensity for classical antiquity is expressed more strongly in his designs for public buildings and the city gates, which he dubbed the "propylaea of Paris." In the house shown here, the great entrance archway is intersected at column level by the ground-floor ceiling, leaving the semicircular window to illuminate the central semicircular landing on the upper floor. This is not a particularly felicitous solution.

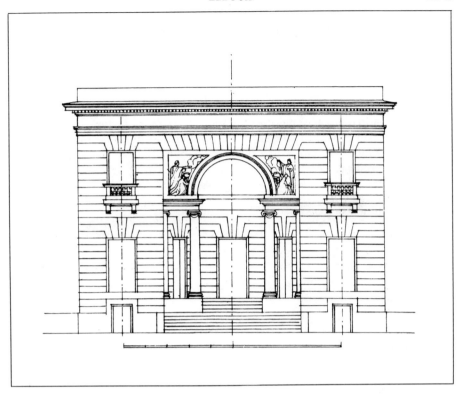

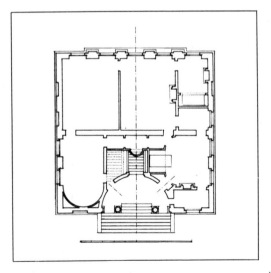

ANCIEN HÔTEL DE M. TABARY, RUE DU FAUBOURG POISSONNIÈRE

Plate XI: Pavillon à Eaubonne
This small house for Monsieur de Mézières is found in Ledoux' collected works and in Krafft's miscellany. Despite the obvious quality of the design, Krafft found that "the house offers nothing worthy of especial note." Indeed, the works of Ledoux were long regarded with indifference and a lack of understanding. Perhaps things might have been different if so many of the buildings he was permitted to realize were not demolished so soon after their construction.

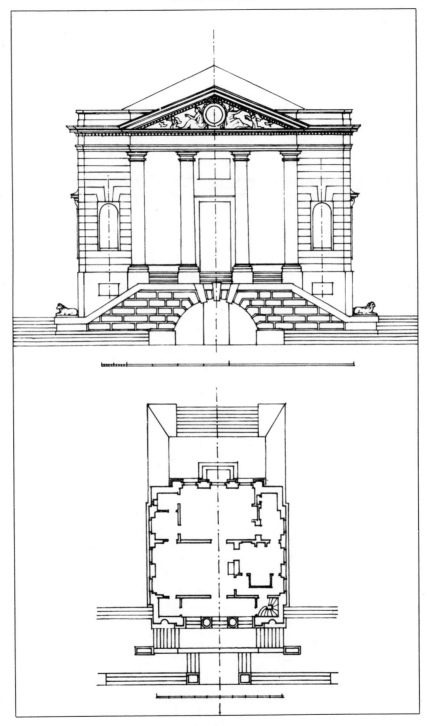

PAVILLON, A EAUBONNE

Plate XII: Pavillon de Louveciennes
This pavilion was commissioned by Madame Du Barry and was erected on a site that enjoyed a distant view of the countryside. Madame Du Barry later commissioned Ledoux to design a chateau for Louveciennes, but this was never built. Louis XV loved this pavilion, which reminded him of Gabriel's Petit Trianon. The pavilion is still standing, although an additional story was subsequently added. (The original notes on Ledoux' biography and on Plates XI and XII have been slightly expanded.)

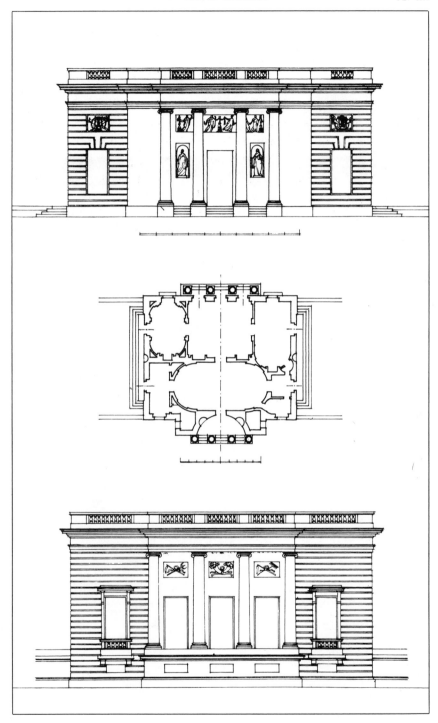

PAVILLON DE MADAME DU BARRY, A LOUVECIENNES

Plate XIII: Pavillon de la Barrière d'Enfer
The pavilion stands on the *Place Denfert-Rochereau* and is one of a pair
of identical pavilions at the head of the *Avenue d'Orléans.* We have already
seen that Ledoux' work was not always well liked, and the view of these
pavilions was that "they did little to the credit of the architect," a judg-
ment that now seems rather hard on Ledoux, since for all their weight
his facades are well proportioned, and the delicacy of the frieze contrasts
pleasingly with the strength of the columns in the plinth. The purpose
of the oval shapes that separate the delicate figures in the frieze, looking
for all the world like so many huge amphorae, is often misunderstood,
but the engravings in Ledoux' work leave us in no doubt that the figures
portray scenes from cities whose coats-of-arms were to have appeared
on these shields. It is not known why this never came about.

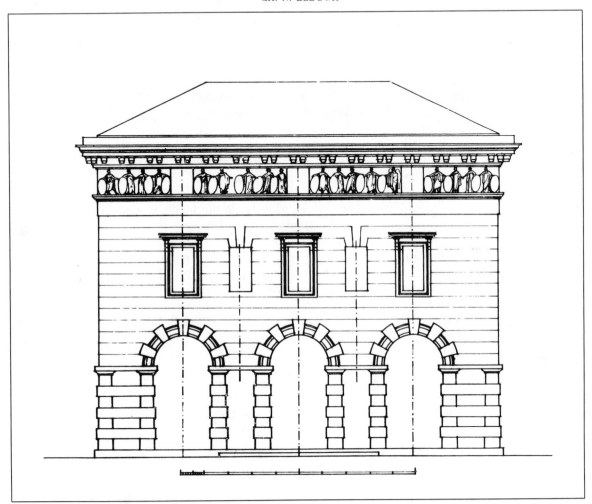

PAVILLONS DE LA BARRIÈRE D'ENFER, A PARIS

Pierre-Charles-Joseph Normand

1765–1840

Born in Guyencourt, Normand was a student of Gisors and won the Grand Prix d'Architecture in 1792. Normand is better known as a copperplate engraver than as an architect. His book *Parallèle d'Ordres* is surely the most important of his published works and is still in use today. The collection from which these plates are taken is called *Recueil Varié* and appeared in 1823. It contains typical ground plans and views for town and country residences, monuments, public works, and special commissions. "The ground plans," according to the author, "suit our modern needs, which are comparable with requirements in other parts of Europe. They can be freely combined with a variety of different facades, be they facades with transverse wings, arcades or colonnades, facades with pillars, buttresses or raised roofs, facades with loggias, verandas, pavilions, fountains or pampres in the Italian manner." The charm of these small, finely engraved designs is evident; errors in scale are only around 1 millimeter per meter, and one must be careful not to destroy their effect when enlarged. The original edition contained 150 illustrations with which Normand claimed to be already familiar, stating that "some are widely scattered throughout Europe." Many of these designs are to be found in a somewhat modified form in the collection of Seheult (see pages 68–75).

Plate XIV: Café dans un Jardin Public.
Normand classifies the "café in a public park" among those designs that "are based upon a composition of verticals such as columns, arcades, or rows of windows."

(Plate 4 in Normand)

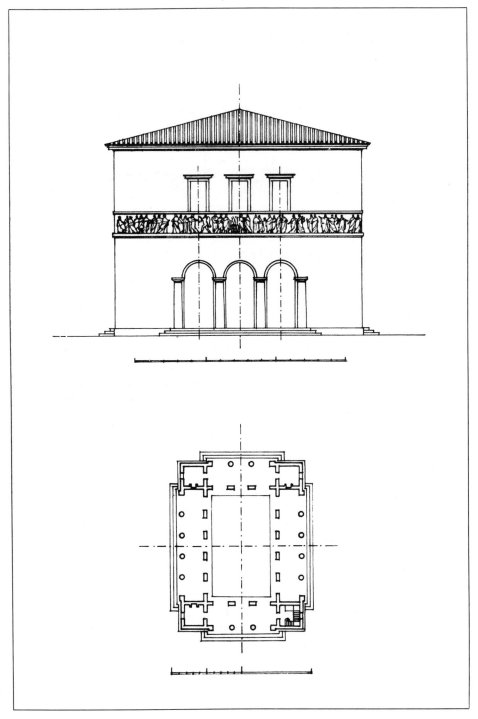

CAFÉ, DANS UN JARDIN PUBLIC

Plate XV: Maison Décorée de Sgraffites
This house, decorated with sgraffiti, contained a vestibule, dining room,
salon, and other apartments.

(Plate 14 in Normand)

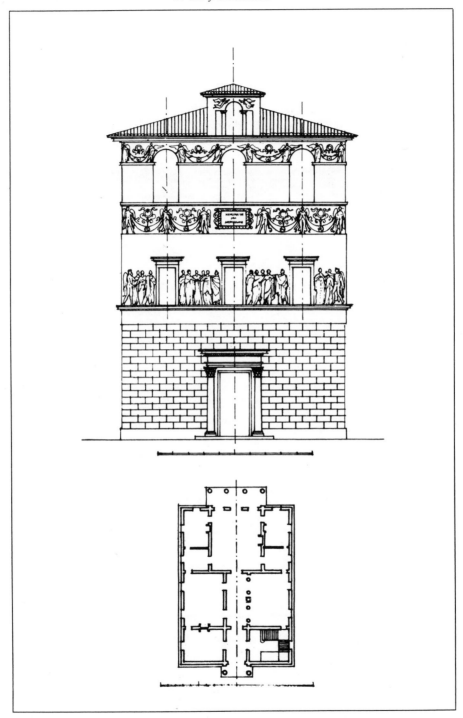

MAISON DÉCORÉE DE SGRAFFITES

Plate XVI: Hôtel Particulier
This private house has a facade adorned with reliefs and statuary. The ground plan encloses an inner courtyard with a colonnade; at the rear are kitchens, offices, stables, and coach houses.

(Plate 2 in Normand)

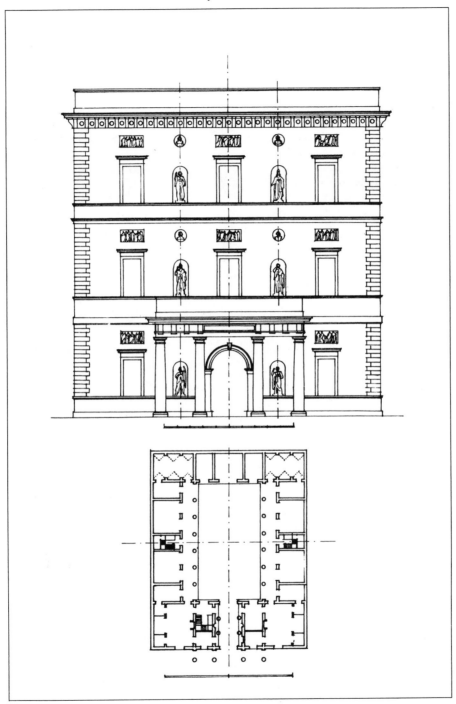

HÔTEL PARTICULIER

Plate XVII: Maisons
Above: the facade of a *Philosopher's House,* which incorporates a vestibule, a chamber illuminated from above, and a number of smaller apartments that "all merge with each other."

(Plate 42 in Normand)

Below: the facade of a *Manufacturer's House* including workshop, hot-house, and storeroom on the ground floor. The facade was apparently inspired by the design of a house on the road to Capua, which Seheult had published in his own collection.

(Plate 17 in Normand)

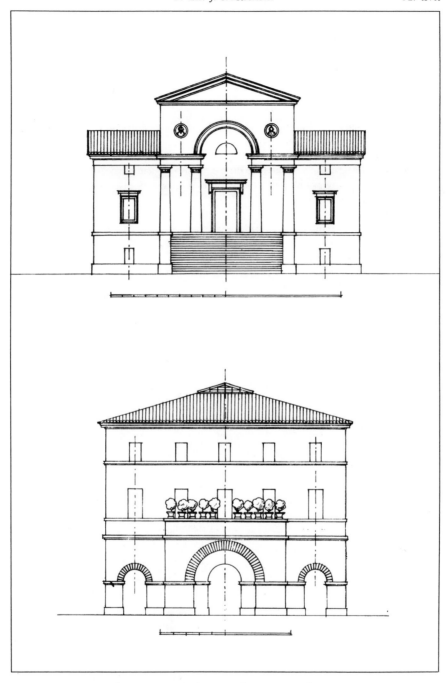

MAISON D'UN PHILOSOPHE (EN HAUT) ET MAISON D'UN FABRICANT

Plate XVIII: Maisons
Left: a design called merely "small house," with vestibule, staircase, salon, dining room, etc.

Right: a design for a "roadside house" with terrace, vestibule, hallway, staircase, dining room, and salon; there are bedrooms upstairs and a kitchen in the basement.

(Plate 41 in Normand)

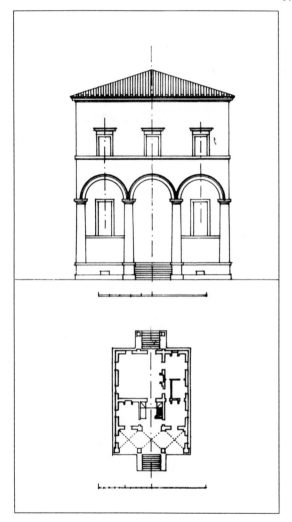

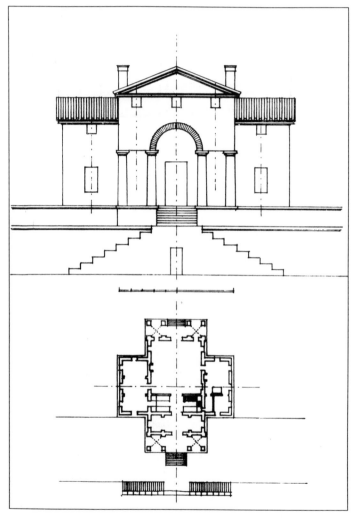

PETITE MAISON   MAISON SUR UNE TERRASSE, AU BORD D'UNE ROUTE

PIERRE-CHARLES-JOSEPH NORMAND

Plate XIX: Maisons
The house on the left belongs to the same series as Plate XVIII and is part of a number of designs that examined the effects of raised entrances and loggias. The design on the right is the *House of an Astronomer* and is one of a series that looked at different roof forms.

(Plate 26 in Normand)

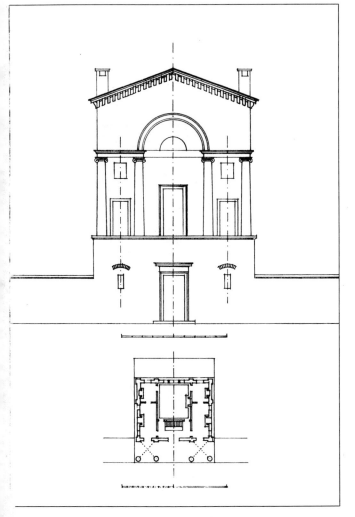

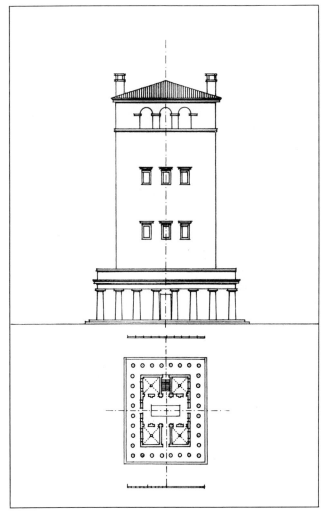

PETITE MAISON AU BORD D'UNE ROUTE   MAISON D'UN ASTRONOME

Plate XX: Maison de Campagne
The two country houses in Plates XX and XXI are among the designs that Normand used to examine the "effect of pampres as decoration for facades." This particular house has an access to the upper terrace, which Normand referred to as a "gradinata à l'Italienne."

(Plate 47 in Normand)

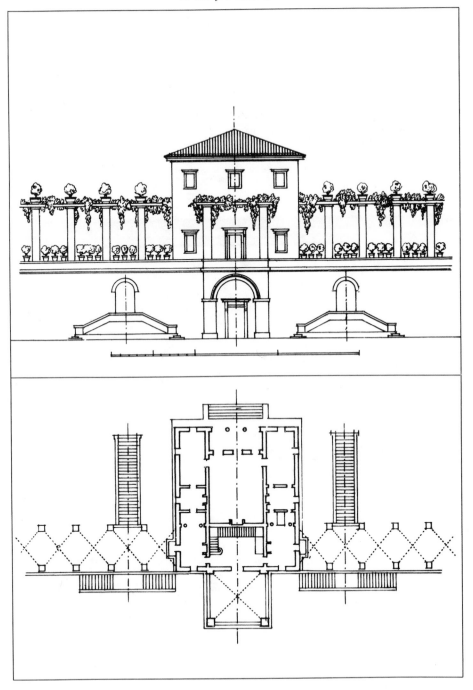

MAISON DE CAMPAGNE AVEC TREILLES

Plate XXI: Maison de Campagne
This small, charming, almost Palladian residence also stands at a roadside and encloses "terrace, garden, hothouses, and a complete dwelling."

(Plate 49 in Normand)

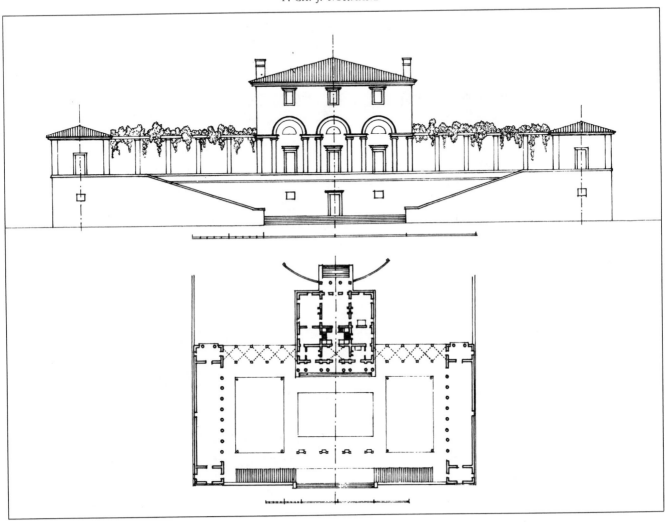

MAISON DE CAMPAGNE, AVEC TREILLES

Plate XXII: Maison de Campagne
This small house is one of the designs with "fountains as adornment to the house." It lies on a road, between courtyard and garden, with two exterior staircases and a central inner staircase, with anteroom, reception room, dining room, salon, and bedrooms above.

(Plate 44 in Normand; Plate 5 shows a very similar house on the road from Rome to Tivoli.)

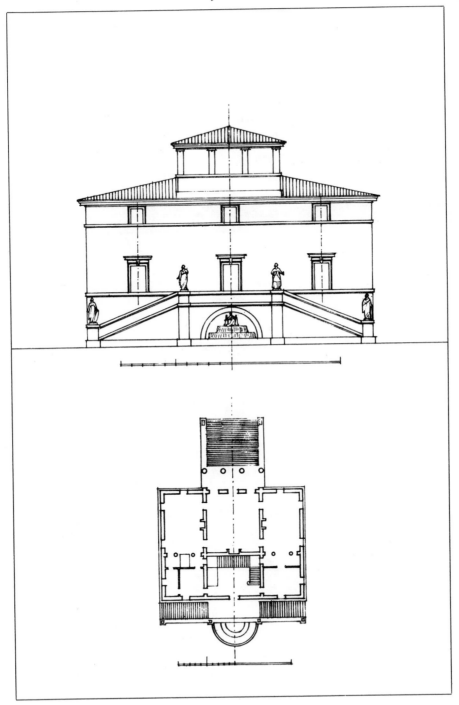

MAISON AVEC BELVÉDÈRE ET GRAND PERRON

Plate XXIII: Maison de Campagne
This house constitutes an "exercise in towers" and contains a vestibule, dining room, billiard room, salon, bedrooms, kitchen, etc.

(Plate 35 in Normand)

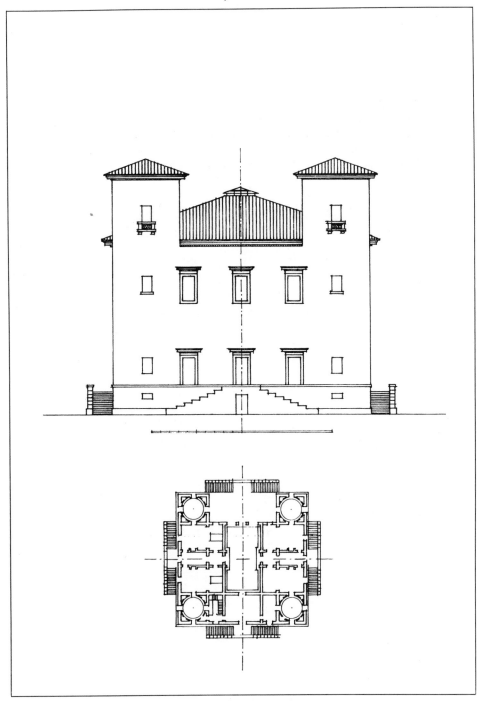

MAISON DE CAMPAGNE, AVEC BELVÉDÈRES

Plate XXIV: Étude pour un Château
Both Plate XXIV and Plate XXV were apparently influenced by the Villa Medici in Rome. The chateau is reminiscent of the garden front, while the design for the small palace is akin to the main entrance front. The two facades belong to different studies in Normand's work.

(Plate 32 in Normand)

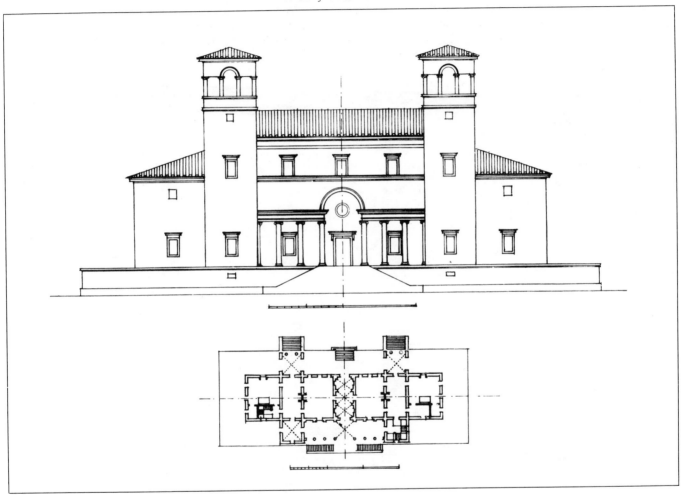

ÉTUDE POUR UN CHÂTEAU

49

Plate XXV: Étude pour un Hôtel ou Petit Palais
A large courtyard with fountain and nymphs, kitchens, administrator's office, outbuildings. Apartments on the first and second floors.

(Plate 34 in Normand)

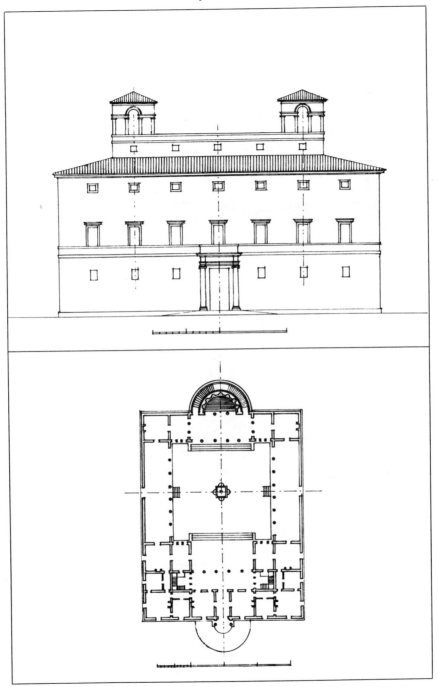

ÉTUDE POUR UN HÔTEL OU PETIT PALAIS

51

Plate XXVI: Villa avec Terrasse et Fontaines
Like Plate XXII, this study belongs to the series of "studies with fountains." It is a country house whose ground floor has been raised one story to improve the view. The residence accommodates anterooms, salon, dining room, and sumptuous bedchambers. The lower ground floor provides space for the less stately apartments.

(Plate 44 in Normand)

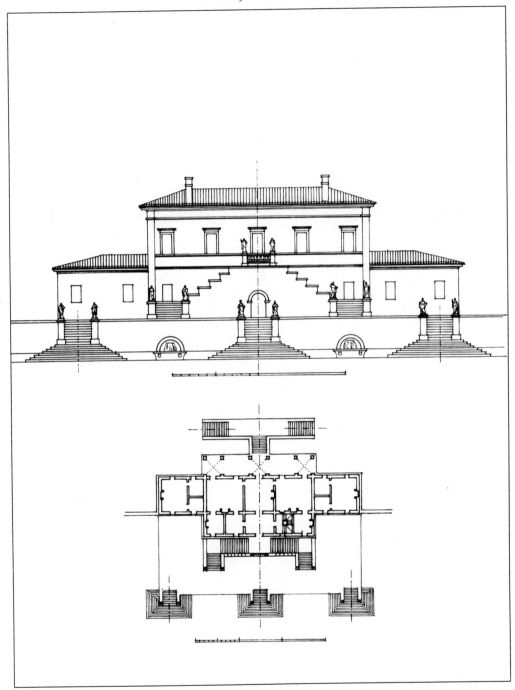

VILLA AVEC TERRASSE ET FONTAINES

Plate XXVII: Ancien Château
This is a study for an old-style chateau. The U-shaped ground plan is traversed by an axis with a staircase at each end.

(Plate 15 in Normand)

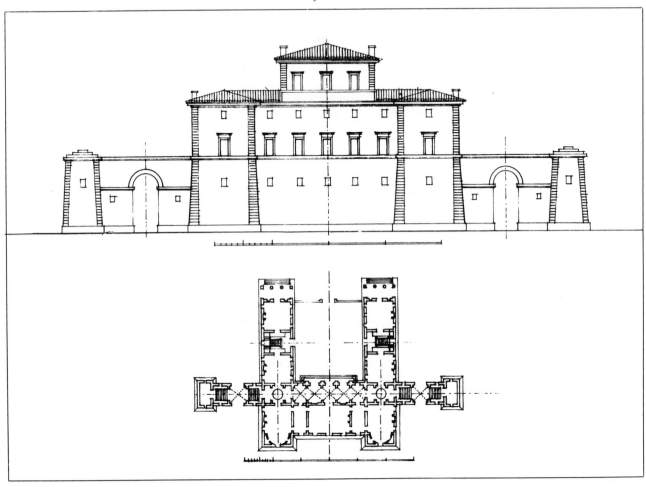

ANCIEN CHÂTEAU

Plate XXVIII: Atelier pour un Menuisier ou un Peintre de Décors
This design for a workshop (for a cabinetmaker or painter) belongs to
Normand's series of studies on roof forms. The facade is really very
simple, and yet it achieves a particular freshness and boldness through
the sheer clarity of the composition.

(Plate 18 in Normand)

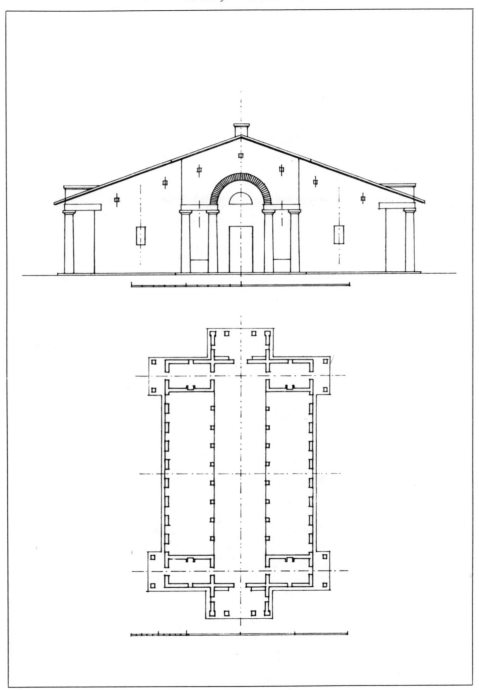

ATELIER POUR UN MENUISIER OU UN PEINTRE DE DÉCORS

Plate XXIX: Construction dans une Fabrique et Halle au Blé pour une Petite Ville
The study on the left Normand calls "part of a window factory with furnaces and glassworks."

The design on the right is a study for the corn market in a small town, incorporating offices, broad staircases, and shops in the upper story.

(Plate 11 in Normand)

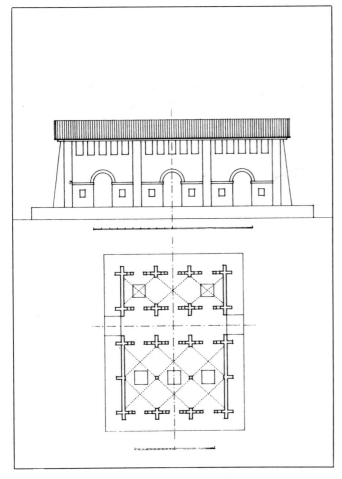

CONSTRUCTION DANS UNE FABRIQUE

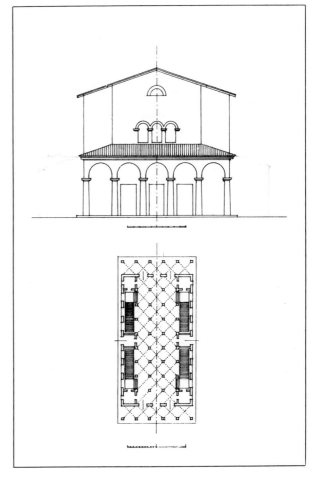

HALL AU BLÉ POUR UNE PETITE VILLE

Plate XXX: Église Paroissiale
This parish church for a small provincial town, with its simple ground plan and facade, is a pure stroke of genius. It is scarcely conceivable that such an astonishing effect could have been achieved with so few means.

(Plate 17 in Normand)

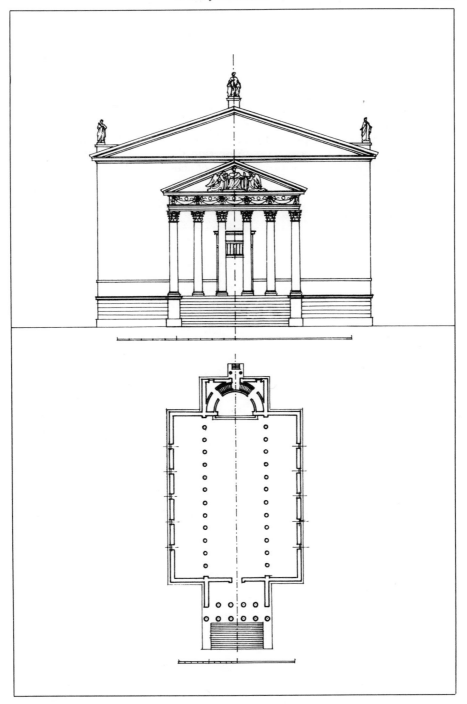

ÉGLISE PAROISSIALE

Plate XXXI: Salle de Spectacle
The ground plan of this multiple-function theater was slightly modified
from another Normand design in order to increase the ancillary areas.
The building houses a lobby, staircase, café, gallery, stalls, orchestra pit,
stage, dressing rooms, and a public foyer above the lobby.

(Plate 50 in Normand)

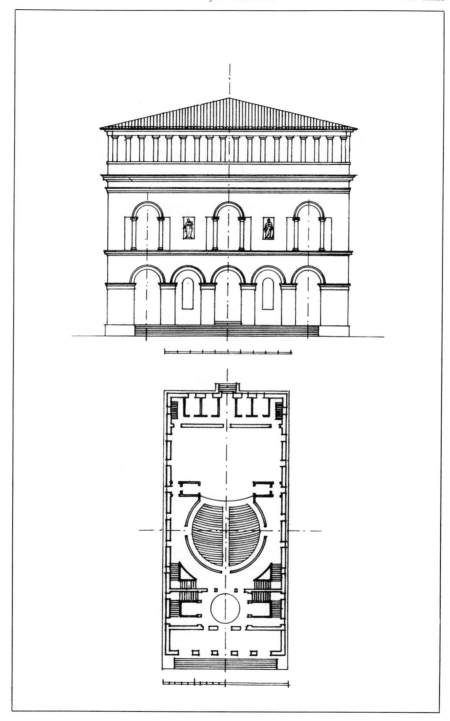

SALLE DE SPECTACLE

Plate XXXII: Project de Bibliothèque pour une Petite Ville
This design for a municipal library is worth comparing with Plate XXX: the entrance facades are equally well proportioned, and here the elegant portico is additionally enhanced by the expanse of bare wall behind. The ground plan is simple without being cold.

(Plate 36 in Normand)

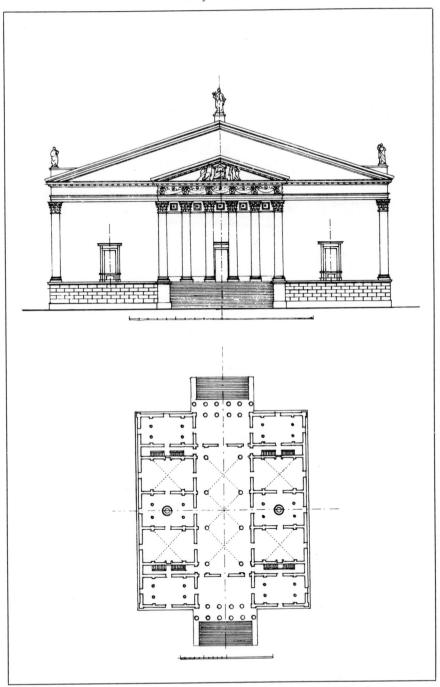

PROJET DE BIBLIOTHÈQUE POUR UNE PETITE VILLE

Charles Percier

1764–1838

Percier was born in Paris and was a pupil of Gisors and Peyre. He was awarded the Prix de Rome in 1786. From 1794 to 1814 he worked together with Pierre François Léonard Fontaine as the architect of Napoleon, and in 1798 the two architects published a joint work on the houses and palaces of Rome, *Palais, Maisons etc. à Rome,* from which Plate XXXIII is taken as typical of the small Roman city mansion.

Plate XXXIII: Petit Palais dans le Faubourg du Peuple, à Rome
Percier tells us that this palace was on the right bank of the Tiber, slightly above the church of Sante Andrea de Vignole and towards Ponte Molle (i.e., on the road out of the city).

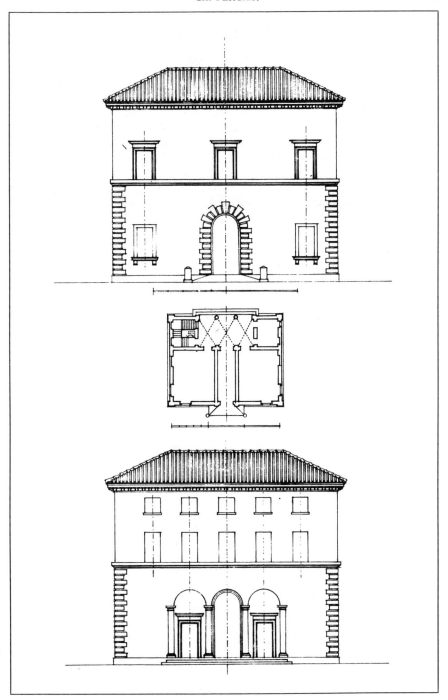

PETIT PALAIS DANS LE FAUBOURG DU PEUPLE, A ROME

François Léonard Seheult

1771–1840

Architect in Nantes. We have already mentioned Seheult's collection in conjunction with the designs of Normand. Seheult himself states that he drew these studies in Italy between 1791 and 1793; they were published in 1811. His decorative detail is perhaps not so finely drawn as that of Normand, but his small houses, usually surrounded by trees and lawns, captivate the onlooker with their simple beauty.

Plate XXXIV: Maisons à Rome sur les Bords du Tibre (en haut) et près du Sainte-Marie du Trastévère
Houses in Rome, the first on the banks of the Tiber, a site that explains its high foundation walls.

(Plate 15 in Seheult)

The second house, just as well proportioned, is not far from Santa Maria de Trastevere. Normand used this facade motif for one of his very small studies.

(Plate 19 in Seheult)

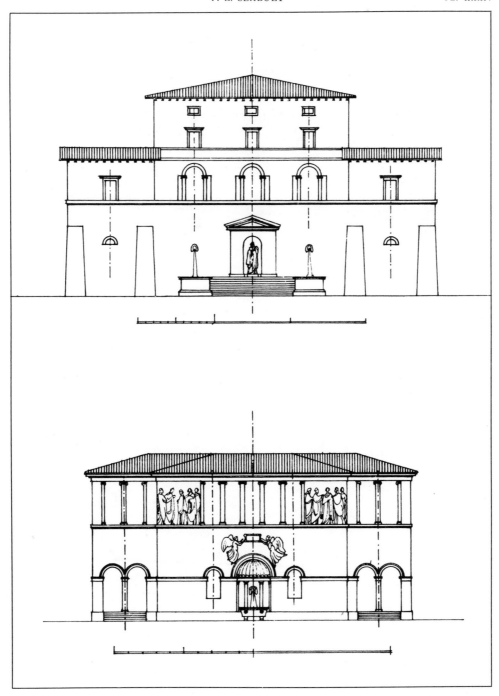

MAISONS A ROME

Plate XXXV: Constructions près de Gaete et au Bord du Tibre
Both of these drawings, variations on a theme, are most impressive.

(Plates 26 and 15 in Seheult)

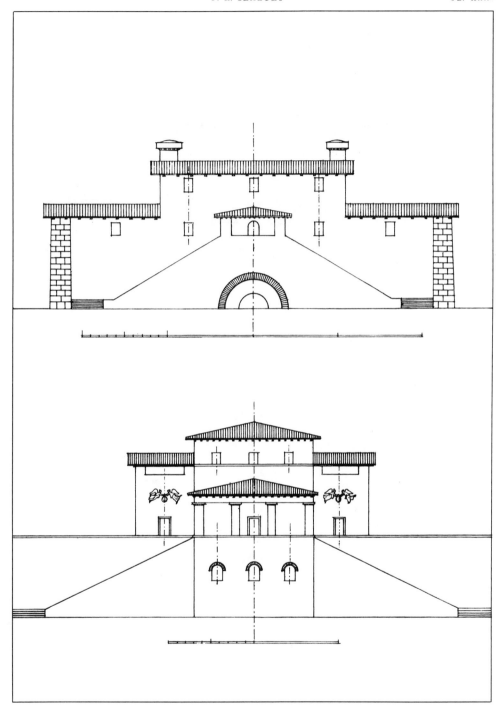

CONSTRUCTIONS
PRÈS DE GAËTE (EN HAUT) ET AU BORD DU TIBRE

Plate XXXVI: Maisons aux Environs de Rome
The house above is on the road from Rome to Tivoli, while the one below, with its large terrace, is on the banks of the Tiber.

(Both Plate 24 in Seheult)

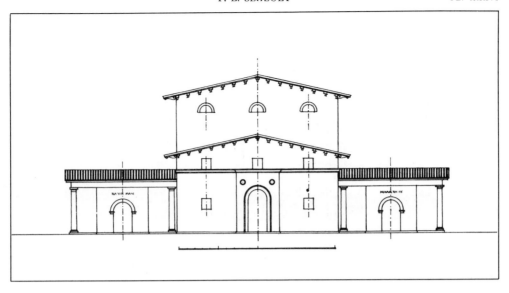

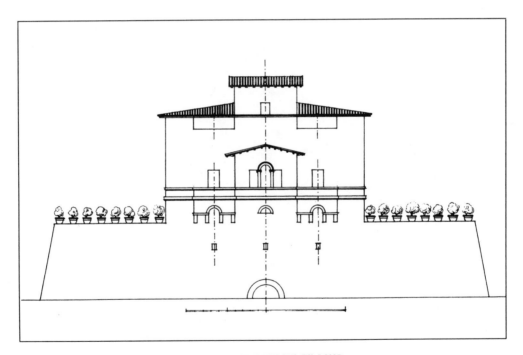

MAISONS AUX ENVIRONS DE ROME
ROUTE DE TIVOLI   ET   SUR LES BORDS DU TIBRE

Plate XXXVII: Maisons à Rome et aux Environs
Seheult tells us that these houses are:

I   in Rome, near the Capitol
II   in Rome, in the "Faubourg du Peuple"
III   on the banks of the Tiber
IV   in the hills of Frascati

(Plates 1, 20, and 24 in Seheult)

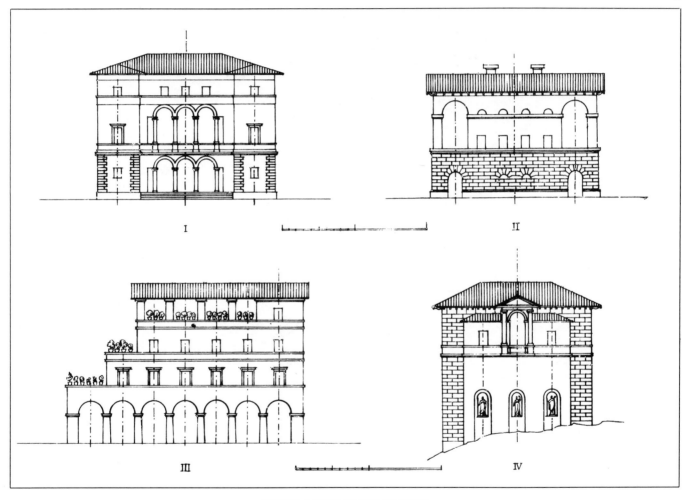

MAISONS A ROME ET AUX ENVIRONS

I. A ROME, PRÈS DU CAPITOLE

II. FAUBOURG DU PEUPLE

III. SUR LES BORDS DU TIBRE

IV. A FRASCATI

Henry van Cleemputte

1792–1860

Van Cleemputte was a student of Percier and apprenticed to his father, who was in turn a pupil of Gabriel. Van Cleemputte worked chiefly as district architect for the department of Manche and later on in Aisne, designing the courthouses of Saint-Lô and Valognes as well as the latter town's theater, the commercial tribunal of Granville, the town hall of Coutances, and the prisons of Coutances and Mortain, etc.

Plate XXXVIII: Tribunal de Saint-Lô, Façade et Plan
The local courthouse, the drawings for which were published by Gourlier in his *Choix d'Édifices Publics,* is typical of public buildings which, though unimposing in size, are nevertheless impressive. The execution of the views displays true skill.

Key to ground plan:

A. Conference room, with area *A* reserved for the public.
B. Council chamber
C. President's chamber
Three rooms—*D, E,* and *F*—are for the court attendants, advocates, and public prosecutors.
L. Two rooms for the concierge, who also has an apartment at ground level.
G. Room for the examining magistrate.
J. Room for the public prosecutor. A room *H*, between *G* and *J*, is reserved for witnesses.
The remand cells are in the rooms marked *K,* and there is a records office on a mezzanine floor reached via a small staircase that can be seen in the ground plan.

The building was erected in 1823.

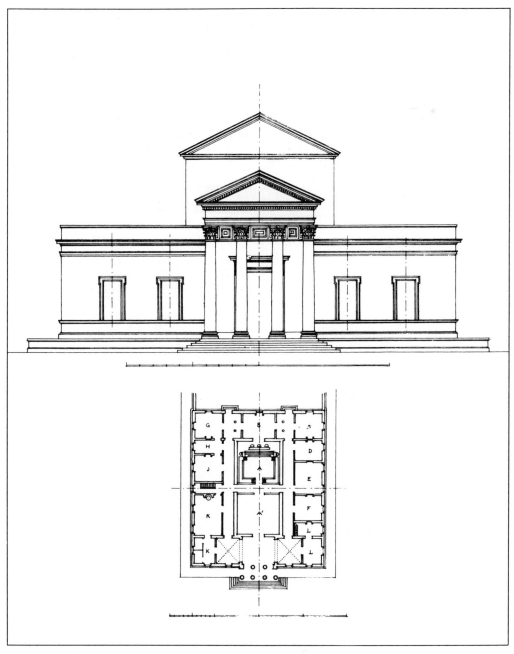

TRIBUNAL DE SAINT-LÔ (1823)
FAÇADE ET PLAN

Plate XXXIX: Tribunal de Saint-Lô
Coupe Longitudinale
This longitudinal section shows the interior layout of the courthouse.
(The cross-section—the last plate in Gromort's collection—has been omitted from the American edition.)

TRIBUNAL DE SAINT-LÔ - COUPE LONGITUDINALE

Index

Page numbers in *italics* refer to figures.

Notes

Notes

Notes